Essential Life Science

VARIATION AND CLASSIFICATION

Melanie Waldron

Raintree is an imprint of Capstone Global Library Limited, a company incorporated in England and Wales having its registered office at 7 Pilgrim Street, London, EC4V 6LB – Registered company number: 6695582

To contact Raintree, please phone 0845 6044371, fax +44 (0)1865 312263, or email myorders@raintreepublishers.co.uk.

First published in hardback in 2014

Edited by Andrew Farrow and Diyan Leake
Designed by Victoria Allen
Original illustrations © Capstone Global Library Ltd 2014
Picture research by Ruth Blair
Production by Sophia Argyris
Originated by Capstone Global Library Ltd
Printed in China by CTPS

ISBN 978 1 406 26232 2
17 16 15 14
10 9 8 7 6 5 4 3 2

British Library Cataloguing in Publication Data
Waldron, Melanie.
Variation and classification. -- (Essential life science)
1. Animals--Classification--Juvenile literature.
2. Plants--Classification--Juvenile literature.
3. Variation (Biology)--Juvenile literature.
I. Title II. Series
570.1'2-dc23

Acknowledgements
We would like to thank the following for permission to reproduce photographs: Alamy pp. 5 (© Corbis Flirt), 18 (© Vincent MacNamara), 26 (© blickwinkel), 37 (© Frans Lemmens; Capstone Publishers (© Karon Dubke) pp. 8, 9, 21, 24, 25, 40, 41); Corbis p. 14 (© Flip Nicklin/Minden Pictures); © Andre Engels p. 36; FLPA p. 43 (Eric Woods); Getty Images pp. 4 (Alexander Safonov), 10 (Rebekka Gudleifsdottir), 13 (Beverly Joubert), 19 (Martin Harvey), 35 (Sylvain Cordier), 42 (Nigel Cattlin); Shutterstock pp. 16 (© cosma), 22 (© Rob kemp), 28 (© RomGams), 30 (© Vlad61), 31 (© Harald Toepfer), 34 (© Richard Whitcombe), 38 (© Jacek Chabraszewski); Superstock pp. 6 (Antoine Juliette/Oredia/Oredia Eurl), 11 (age fotostock), 12 (Minden Pictures), 20 (Cultura Limited), 29 (Minden Pictures), 32 (Minden Pictures).

Cover photograph of tropical fish on a coral reef reproduced with permission of Corbis (© Tischenko Irina).

Every effort has been made to contact copyright holders of material reproduced in this book. Any omissions will be rectified in subsequent printings if notice is given to the publisher.

Contents

What lives on Earth? 4

What is variation? 6

What is evolution? 14

What is classification? 18

How can plants be classified? 26

How are animals classified? 30

How can we identify species? 36

What's next for life on Earth? 42

Glossary 44

Find out more 46

Index 48

Eureka moment!

Learn about important discoveries that have brought about further knowledge and understanding.

DID YOU KNOW?

Discover fascinating facts about variation and classification.

WHAT'S NEXT?

Read about the latest research and advances in essential science.

Some words are shown in bold, **like this**. You can find out what they mean by looking in the glossary.

What lives on Earth?

How many different types of living thing – both plants and animals – do you think there are on Earth? Would you believe that across the world there are millions of different living things? Each different type of plant or animal is called a species. What is even more amazing is that new species are being discovered every year.

Living differences

Everything on Earth is either living or non-living. To stay alive, all living things need a source of energy, such as food. They also need **oxygen**, found in air and water. Apart from this, there are differences between living things. These differences can be tiny, but they can also be huge.

DID YOU KNOW?

Scientists know about and have named around two million different species of plants and animals. However, some people estimate that there may be between three and 100 million species on Earth!

All the living things in this picture need energy and oxygen to stay alive.

Groups of living things

We can look at how living things are different. This is called **variation**. We can try to group similar living things together. This is called **classification**. All living things can be split into five main groups. Animals and plants are the two main groups that this book will focus on. Fungi are a bit like plants, and include mushrooms and toadstools. Protists and bacteria make up the last two groups. These tiny, microscopic living things are found all over the world, in the air, soil, and water.

All humans are the same species. But there are differences, or variations, between us all.

What is variation?

Variation is how things are different. Just think of all the plants and animals you know, and what makes them different from each other. Animals can have two legs, four legs, or no legs. Some have fur, some have scales. Some plants have yellow flowers and some have red flowers.

All of these living things are different because they are different species. However, even things that are the same species can look different. All humans are the same species, but nearly all of us look different. Sometimes twins can look very similar.

All of these children have the same mother and father. Yet they are all different. This is because of variation.

Inherited variations

Some variations – for example, your height or the shape of your ear lobes – are inherited. This means that you get these **traits** from your parents. Parents pass on their **genes** to their children. Genes are the pieces of information inside all your body parts that tell your body what to be like. Since you get a mix of your mother's and your father's genes, your traits will be a mix of theirs. This is the same for all animals and plants.

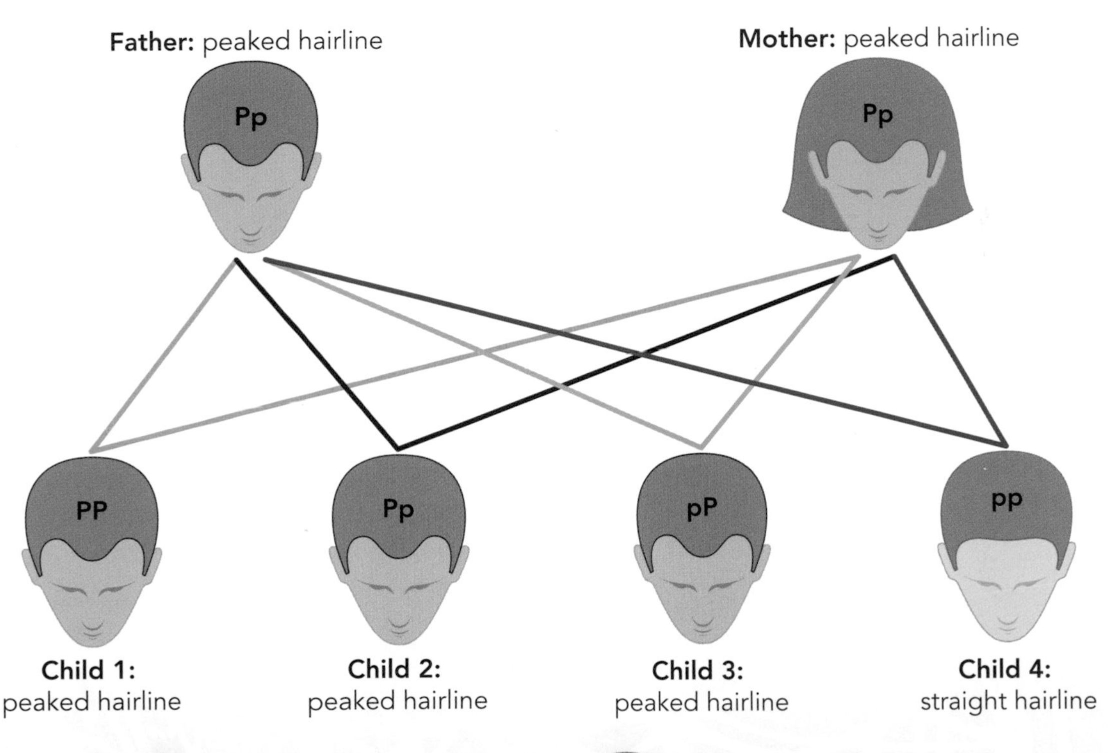

 **P** = gene for peaked hairline

 **p** = gene for straight hairline

In this diagram, each child gets one "hairline" gene from each parent. There can be four combinations, and this will decide what each child's hairline will be like.

Eureka moment!

Gregor Mendel was a scientist. In the 1860s, he was the first person to say that the results of his experiments were because of inherited traits. He did not experiment using humans, though – he used pea plants!

Try this!

Continuous variation means that there will be a wide range of differences in one species. You can see this if you look at the height of people within a group, for example.

Prediction

Children of similar ages are not all the same height. Their heights will show a continuous variation.

What you need

- a tape measure
- a height chart
- a pencil
- a piece of paper
- as many pupils in one year group at school as possible

What you do

1. Measure the heights of all the pupils in the year group. Do this by asking them to stand straight, with their backs against the wall, where the height chart is.

2. Write down each pupil's height on a piece of paper.

3. List all the heights in order, from smallest to tallest. This may be easier to do on a computer, using a spreadsheet.

4. Now plot your results on a bar graph. Put the heights along the horizontal axis, or x-axis. Label the vertical axis, or y-axis, from 0 to 10. If some people are the same height, make the bar taller, depending on how many people are that height.

Conclusion

Your results will show that there is a range of heights, from the smallest to the tallest. This is because height is a continuous variation. Most people will be towards the middle of the range. Does your bar graph show this?

Different variations

Plants and animals of the same species can be different because of the **environment** they live in. For example, hydrangeas are plants with big flowers. The colour of the flowers depends on the type of soil the plant is growing in. Horses living in cold countries will grow much thicker coats than horses living in hot countries.

Learning differently

Many animals can learn different things. For example, sea otters can learn to break open shells using stones. People can learn to speak different languages. You can learn to ski, write, or ride a bicycle. These are all learned traits – you don't inherit them from your parents' genes.

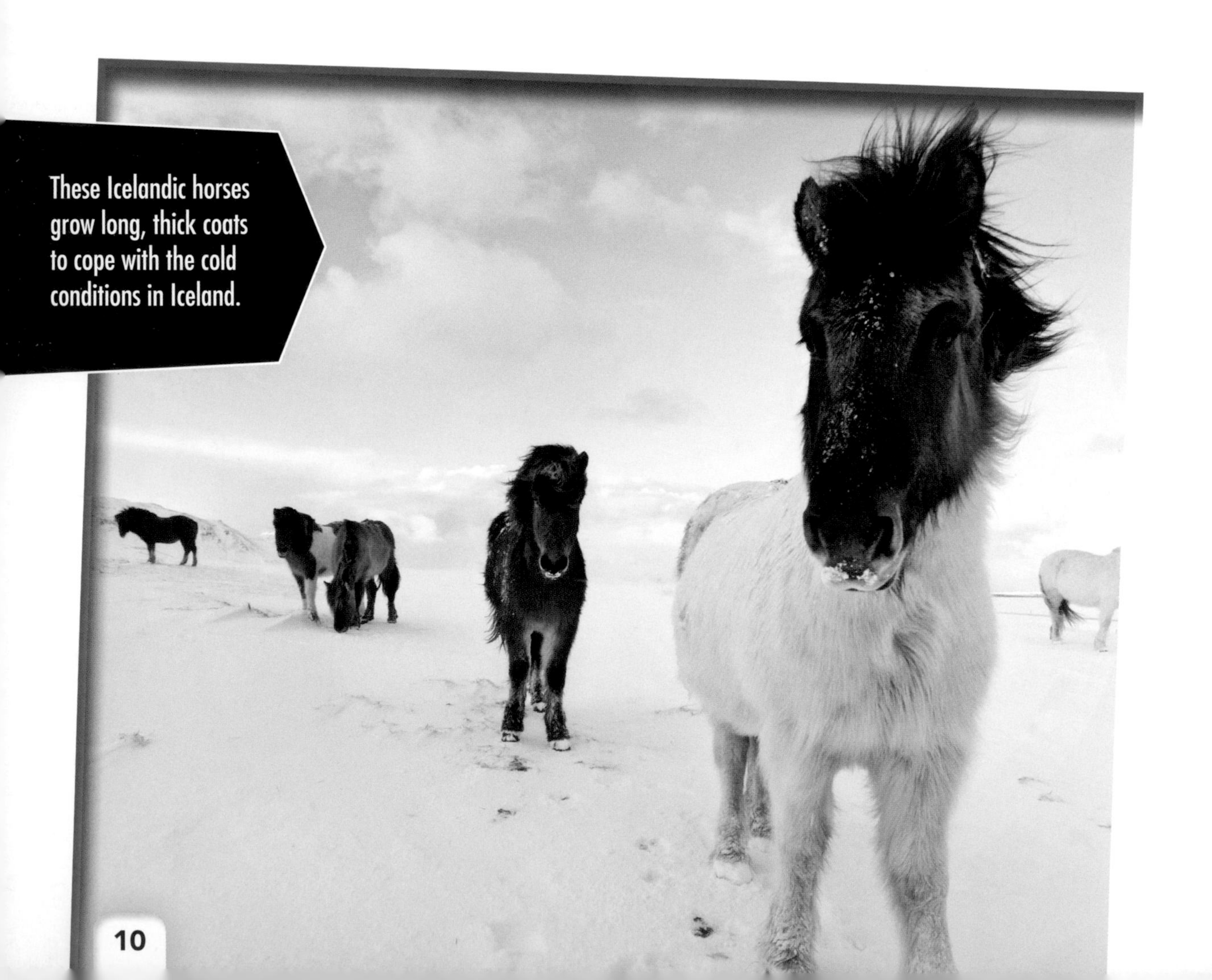

These Icelandic horses grow long, thick coats to cope with the cold conditions in Iceland.

DID YOU KNOW?

You might think that identical twins would look exactly the same, because they share exactly the same mix of their parents' genes. But things like the amount of time they spend in the Sun, or the facial expressions they make, can end up making slight changes to their faces.

Different behaviours

Plants and animals in different **habitats** and environments can behave differently. For example, springtime daffodils growing in southern parts of the United Kingdom will come into flower sooner than those in northern parts. This is because they respond to warm temperatures, and southern areas are usually warmer earlier in the year than northern areas.

Crops that are sprayed with pesticides and fertilizers, and watered in dry weather, will grow much better than the same plants in the wild.

Natural selection

Sometimes plants or animals have variations which make them better suited to their environment than others. For example, imagine two stick insects, each a slightly different shade of green. One shade of green might blend in better with the plants they live on. This would mean that the other one would be slightly easier to spot amongst the plants, and would therefore be the first to get eaten by **predators**.

The insect with better camouflage would live longer, so would be able to have more **offspring**. Eventually all the less well camouflaged stick insects would die out. This process is called **natural selection**.

When this leafy sea dragon is hiding among seaweed, it is difficult for predators to spot it, and so it avoids being eaten.

The fittest

Natural selection means that variations will give some plants and animals a better chance of survival than others. They will live longer and will have more offspring. This is also called survival of the fittest.

Over a long period of time, with natural selection, plants and animals can gradually change so that they become best suited to their environment. This means that different environments will have different plants and animals living there.

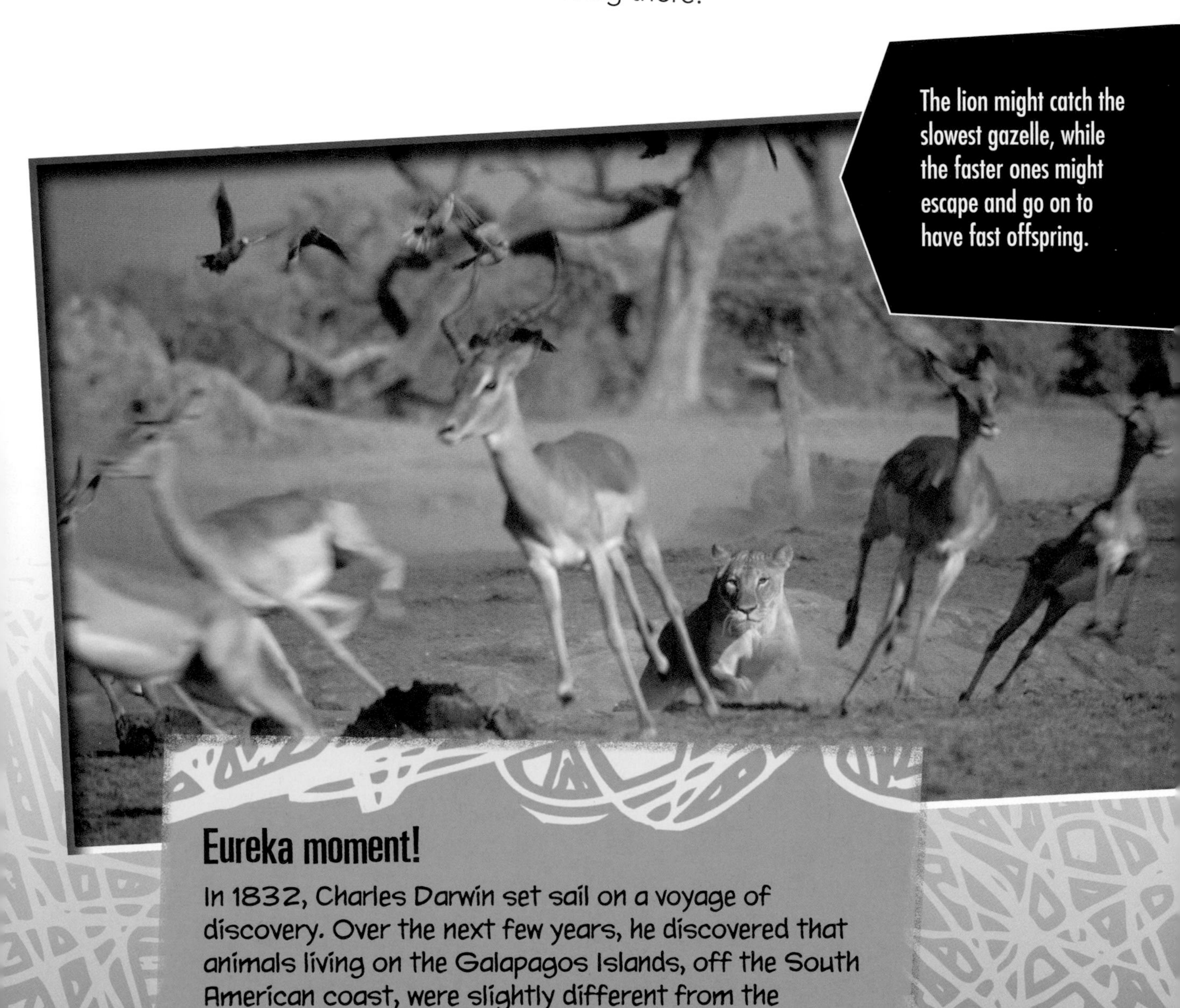

The lion might catch the slowest gazelle, while the faster ones might escape and go on to have fast offspring.

Eureka moment!

In 1832, Charles Darwin set sail on a voyage of discovery. Over the next few years, he discovered that animals living on the Galapagos Islands, off the South American coast, were slightly different from the similar animals on the mainland. He suggested natural selection to explain these differences.

What is evolution?

Evolution is the name given to the very slow process, over thousands of years, in which plants and animals change to become more and more different from each other. Eventually they change so much that they become different species.

Evolution begins with natural selection. Plants or animals with traits best suited to their environments will survive better. These traits will be passed on to their offspring in the genes from the parents. This happens again and again, with tiny differences in traits passing down from parent to offspring, then to their offspring, and so on. Over a long period of time, all these tiny differences will add up to a large difference, and the result will be that a new species has evolved.

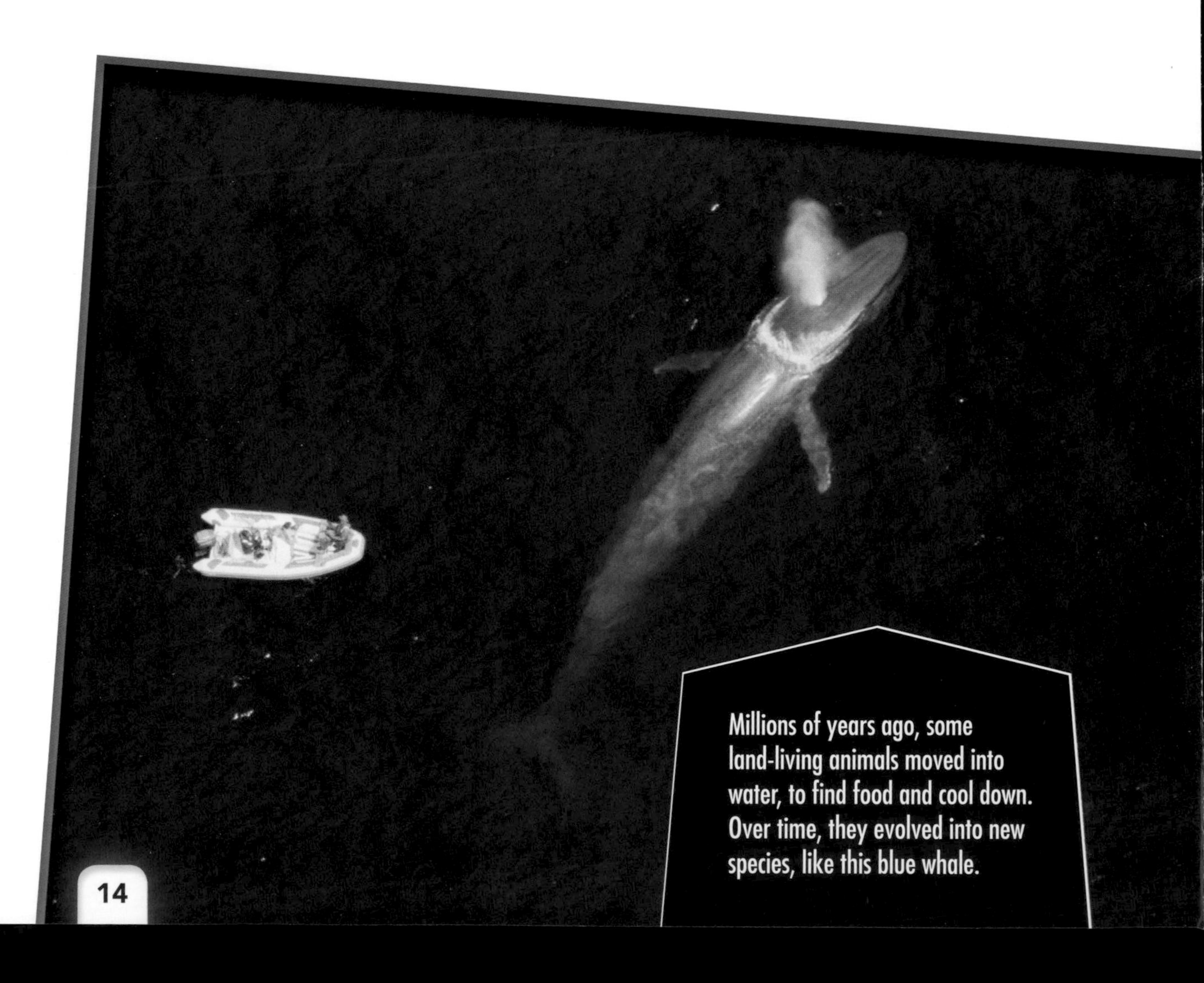

Millions of years ago, some land-living animals moved into water, to find food and cool down. Over time, they evolved into new species, like this blue whale.

Evolving bears

Polar bears are a different species from brown bears. Scientists think that this split first happened about 500,000 years ago. Brown bears living around the Arctic gradually evolved over time and became a new species – polar bears – that were far better suited to living in snowy conditions than brown bears.

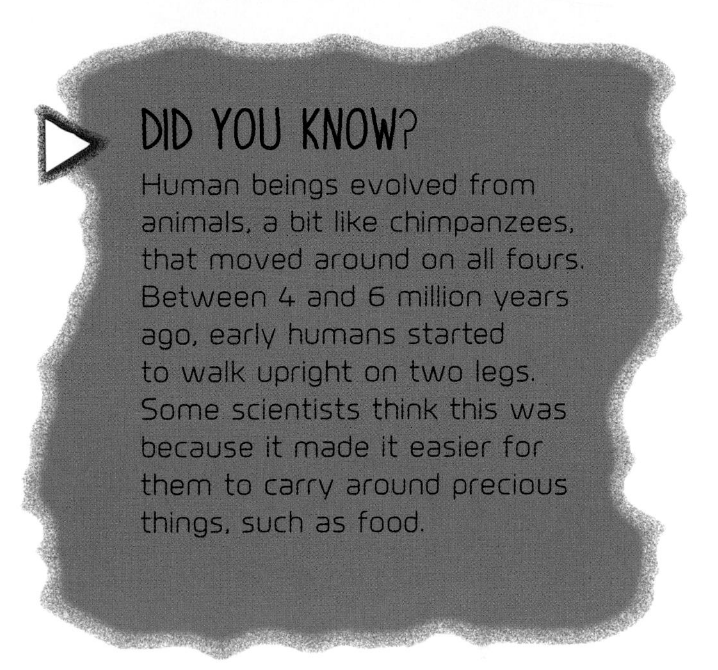

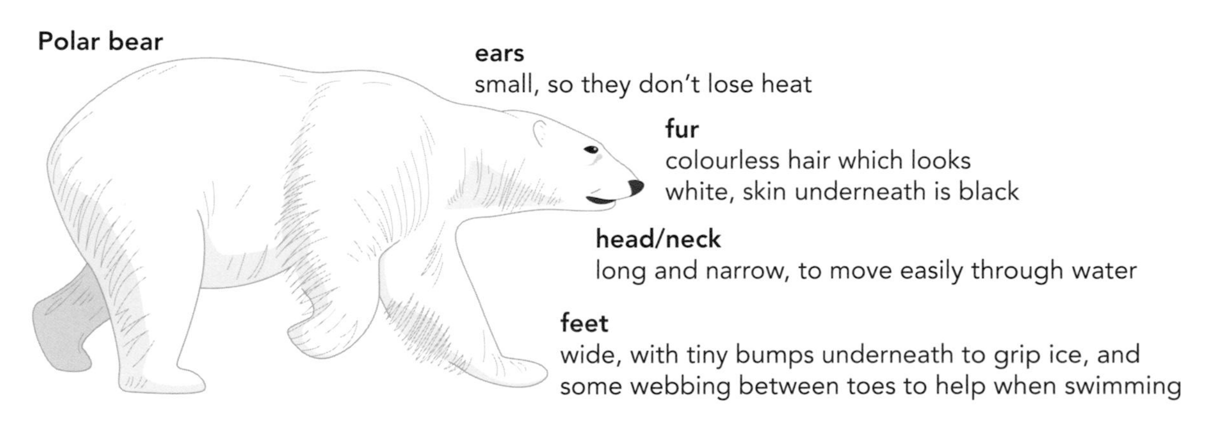

upright height (male): 2–3.4 metres (7–11 feet)
weight (male): 330–600 kilograms (660–1,320 pounds)

upright height (male): 1.5–2.7 metres (5–9 feet)
weight (male): 180–770 kilograms (400–1,700 pounds)

How do we know about evolution?

Fossils show us that plants and animals have evolved and changed over time. They are the remains of plants and animals that lived hundreds of thousands of years ago. They are different from the plants and animals alive today. Scientists can work out how old fossils are, so we know which ones were alive at different times through Earth's history. Today's elephants are part of a group called Proboscidea. There are fossils of animals that are also in the Proboscidea group. The name means that they have trunks.

This is a fossil of a type of lizard that lived long ago.

Extinction

At some times in Earth's history, the environment changed a lot over a short period of time. This led to many species becoming **extinct**, because they could not evolve in time to cope with the changes.

For example, around 65 million years ago, dinosaurs existed. Then something disastrous happened, possibly a huge asteroid hitting Earth. This would have caused the skies to become full of dust and ash. The Sun's light would have been blocked out, and plants would not have been able to grow well. There would have been less food for animals as a result. Also, the dust and ash would have trapped Earth's heat, causing temperatures to soar. However, some living things managed to survive and continued to evolve. These included small, bird-like dinosaurs, shrew-like **mammals**, turtles, snails, and some plants.

WHAT'S NEXT?

There have been five major mass extinctions in Earth's history – when dramatic events have wiped out huge numbers of species. Some people are now worried that human activities may cause the sixth mass extinction.

The mass extinction 65 million years ago killed off most animals and plants.

What is classification?

Evolution over millions of years has led to a huge number of species of plants and animals on Earth. To make it easier to understand them and study them, scientists put them into groups so that similar living things are in similar groups. This is called classification. Things in a group have similar traits or characteristics.

Different species can belong to the same group, if they have similar characteristics. For example, giraffes, pigs, hippopotamuses, camels, and antelopes are all different species. However, they all have four legs, hooves split into two parts, and tails. They all belong to a group called even-toed ungulates.

Cows and sheep both have hooves split in two, four legs, and a tail. Yet they are clearly different species!

Ancestors

When animals share some characteristics, like the even-toed ungulates, it often means that they have the same **ancestors**. This means that millions of years ago they evolved from the same animals. Over time, they all developed their own characteristics, making them all different species, but they still share some other characteristics.

Humans and chimpanzees are descended from the same group of animals. Around 7 to 10 million years ago, the group split and human-like animals started to evolve.

Eureka moment!

In 2002, researchers in Chad in Africa found fossil remains of a very ancient human ancestor. The bones are around 6 to 7 million years old. From studying the bones, scientists think that this early human walked on two legs.

Classification systems

Humans have classified things for thousands of years. Even sorting wild animals into those that might eat you and those that won't is a useful classification! Grouping together plants that are safe to eat, or animals that are easy to hunt, would have helped humans to survive thousands of years ago.

You can classify things in lots of different ways. For example, you could sort animals into groups according to the number of legs they have, or their colour. However, a **classification system** is only really useful if you want other people to be able to understand and use it, too.

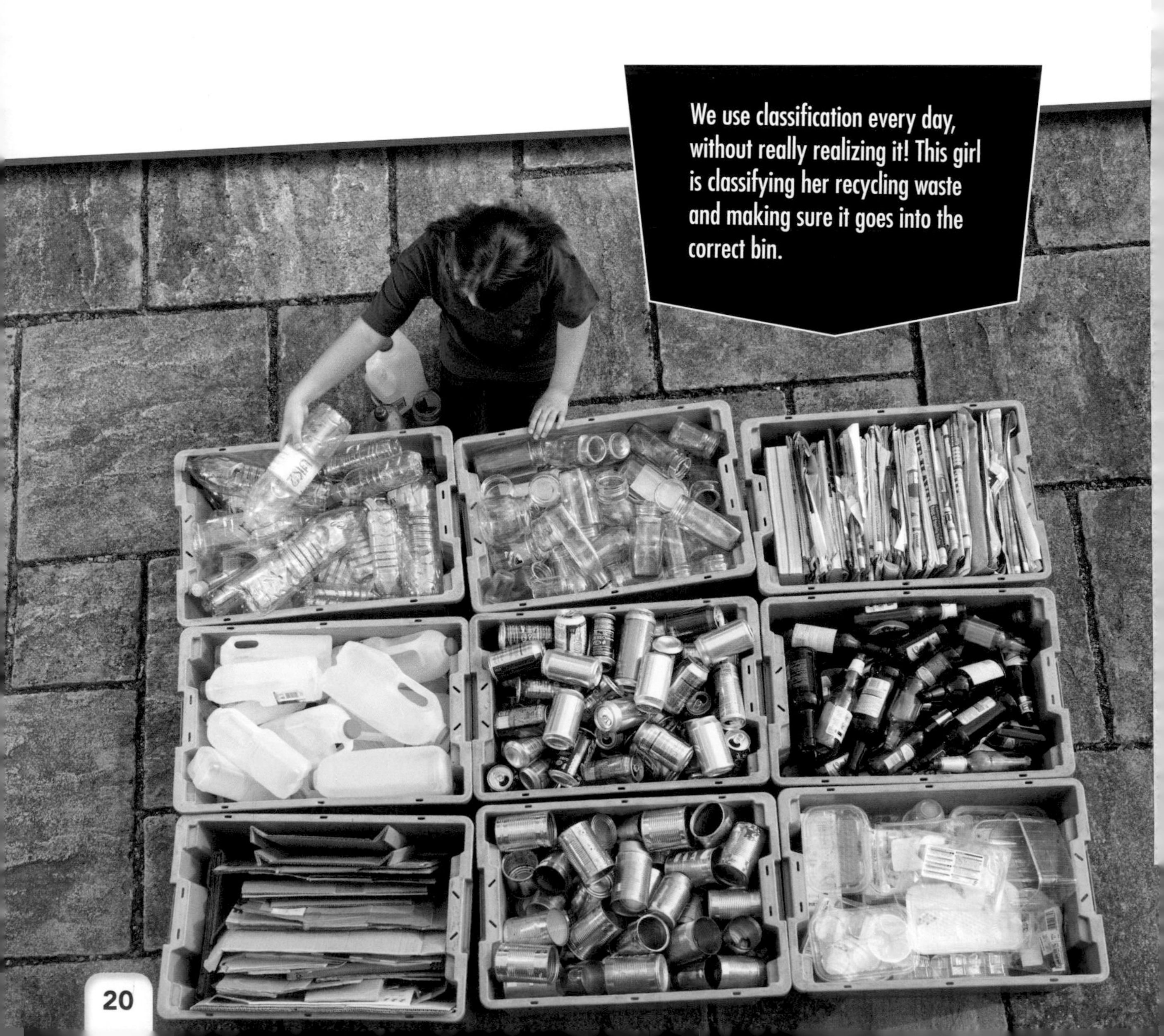

We use classification every day, without really realizing it! This girl is classifying her recycling waste and making sure it goes into the correct bin.

Latin names

Today, scientists across the world still use the classification system drawn up by the Swedish scientist in the 1700s. The system uses Latin words to name things. This gets round the problem of language in different countries or areas. For example, in the United Kingdom we use the name *poppy* for a lovely red flower, but in Spain these flowers are called *amapolas*. This is confusing, but the Latin name for the flower, *Papaver rhoeas*, is the same whichever country you are in.

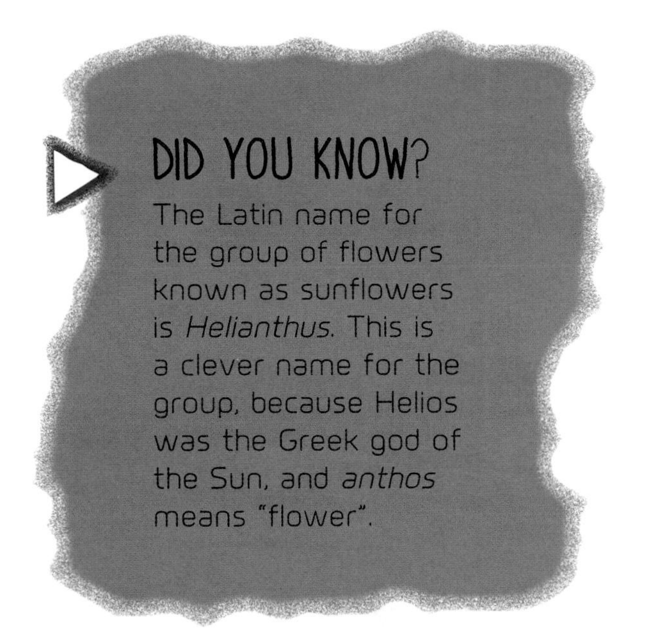

DID YOU KNOW?

The Latin name for the group of flowers known as sunflowers is *Helianthus*. This is a clever name for the group, because Helios was the Greek god of the Sun, and *anthos* means "flower".

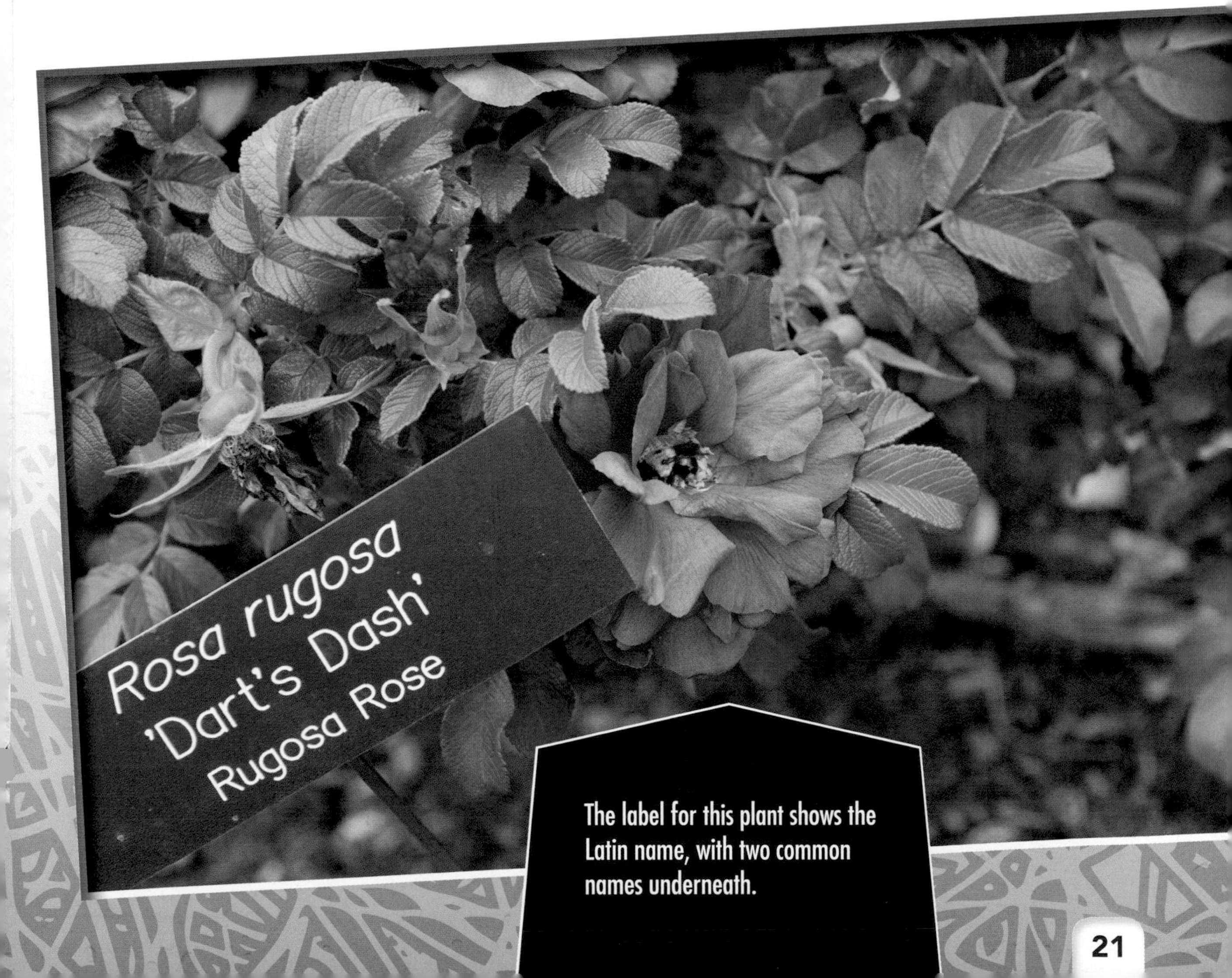

The label for this plant shows the Latin name, with two common names underneath.

Sometimes males and females of one species can look very different. The brightly coloured bird is a male pheasant. The other is a female pheasant.

What is a species?

A species is a single kind of plant or animal, with the same set of characteristics. The main thing that makes something a separate species is that a male and female of one species can come together to have offspring.

Some species – for example, dogs – can be split up into different **breeds**. Breeds are still the same species, so different breeds can still produce offspring. Sometimes people decide which traits they want for their **domestic animals**, such as sheep or cows. They select the male and female with the best traits, and the offspring will also have these traits. This is called selective breeding.

Levels of classification

There are different levels of classification. A very simple classification would be to sort things into living and non-living groups. Living things can then be split into huge groups called **kingdoms**.

Each kingdom can then be divided into smaller groups called phyla. Phyla can be divided into groups called classes, then into orders, families, **genera**, and eventually species. Every kind of plant or animal can be named as an individual species.

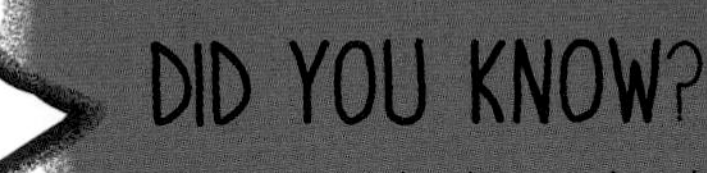

Humans belong to the order called Primates. This group also includes lemurs, lorises, tarsiers, monkeys, and apes! In fact, there are over 300 species in this order. All primates have thumbs, which means they can grasp things in their hands. Can you think of any other similarities?

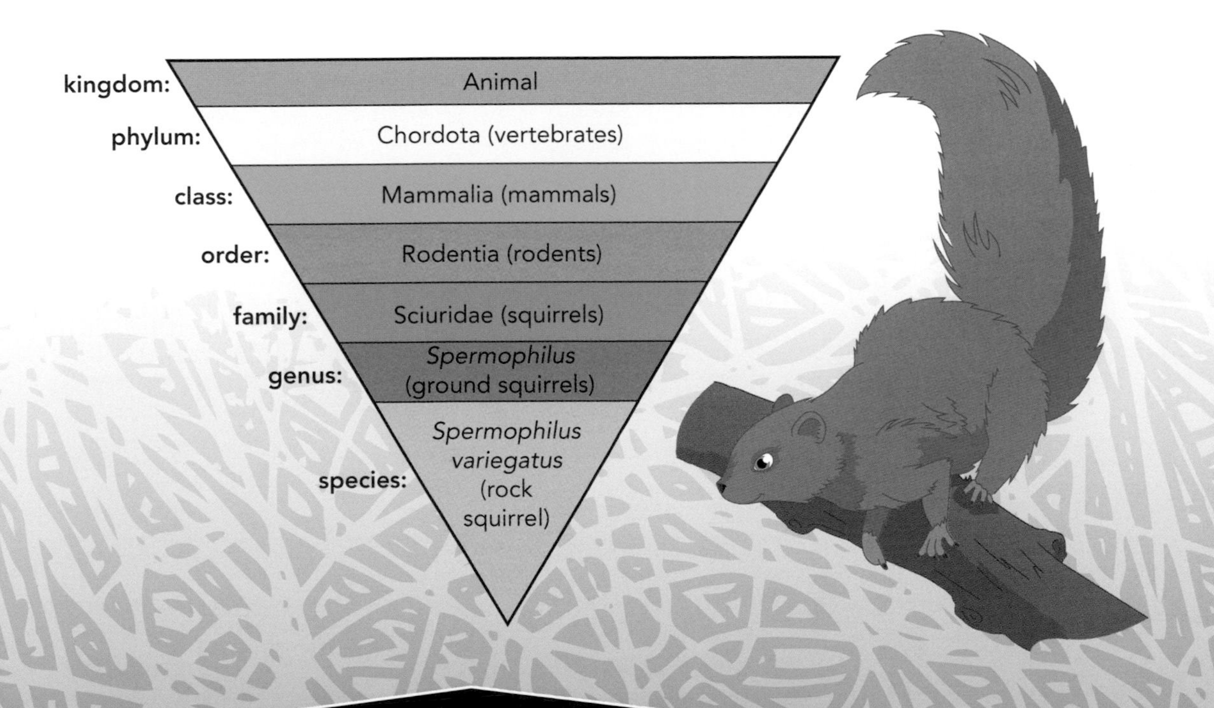

This pyramid shows the classification for the rock squirrel. The pyramid narrows as it goes down through the levels. This shows that there are fewer and fewer animals in each level. In the bottom level, there is only one species, the rock squirrel.

Try this!

You can use a classification system to classify many things – not just plants or animals!

Prediction

I can create a classification system for a set of objects. If I explain my classification system, other people will be able to use it to classify the same objects in the same way.

What you need

Any number of different, non-living items: pen, sock, stone, cotton wool, soft toy, hat, mug, necklace, coin, ball, watch, cushion, phone, spoon, facecloth, glove

What you do

1. Set all of your objects out on a large table.

2. Decide how you might split your objects into groups. You could start by splitting them into two groups: "hard" and "soft". Every time you split groups, remember to write down how you decided to split them.

3 Now look at each group in turn. How can you split them further? You could split the hard objects into two further groups: "objects that need power" and "objects that don't need power". How could you split the soft objects?

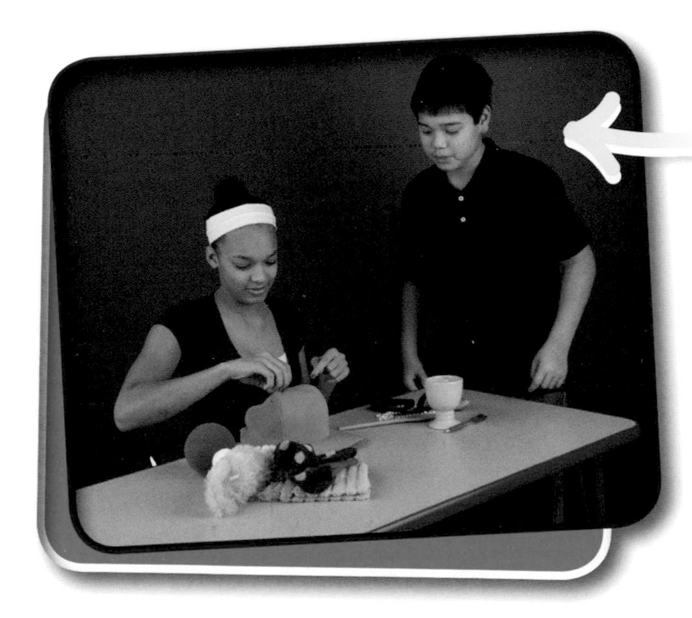

4 Keep going with each smaller and smaller group of objects. Once you have finished, put the objects back together into one group. Now ask another pupil to sort the objects, using the groupings you made. Ask them to do it in the same order that you did it in.

5 Once your friend has finished, look at the objects. Have they been sorted into the same final groups as when you did the sorting?

Conclusion

If your group descriptions were very clear and careful, other people were able to sort the objects in exactly the same way as you did. Your classification system worked!

How can plants be classified?

The plant kingdom is one of the five major groups of living things. Plants have some very basic differences from animals. They can't move around like animals can, and they don't have brains and nerves that control their parts.

The main characteristic of plants is that they can make food for themselves, usually inside their leaves. They do this using the Sun's light, water, and a gas from the air called carbon dioxide. This process of making food is called photosynthesis. Because plants don't need another food source and they produce their own food, they are called producers.

DID YOU KNOW?

Plants growing in rainforests provide us with many things, including timber, coffee, and cocoa. Some of them also contain chemicals that are used to treat diseases such as cancer. Over 2,000 rainforest plants contain anti-cancer chemicals.

Plants create oxygen during photosynthesis. Both plants and animals need oxygen to stay alive.

Groups of plants

The plant kingdom can be split into two groups: vascular plants and non-vascular plants. Vascular plants have little tubes running through their roots, stems, and leaves. These tubes carry water, food, and chemicals from the soil, called nutrients, to all the plant's parts.

Non-vascular plants don't have tubes inside them. They all live in damp or wet places, so all of their parts can take in water and nutrients. Because all their parts need to be damp or wet, non-vascular plants are usually much smaller than vascular plants.

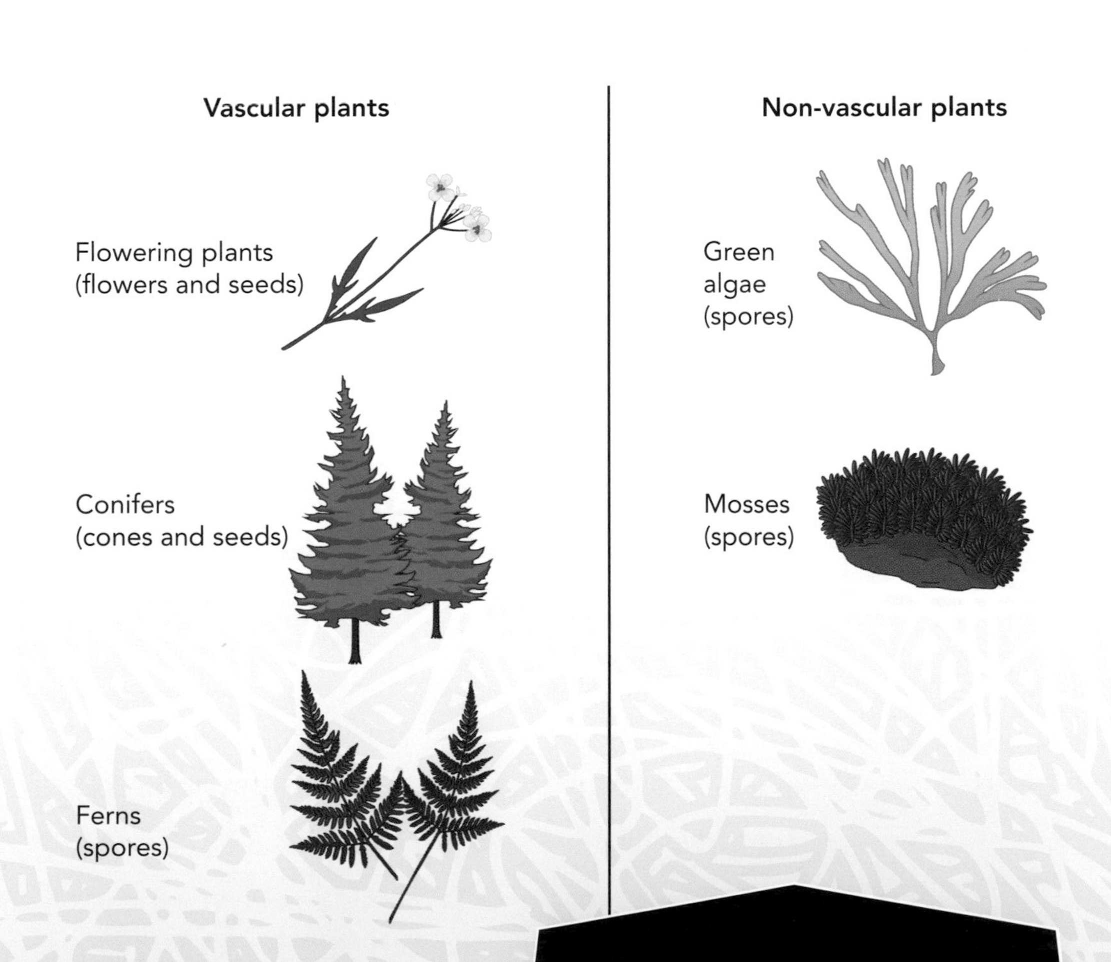

This diagram shows how plants can be classified. There are three groups of vascular plants, and two groups of non-vascular plants.

Vascular plants

There are three main groups of vascular plants: flowering plants, conifers, and ferns. Ferns are leafy plants that don't have flowers or make seeds. They make new plants from tiny balls called spores on their leaves. These blow off the leaves and grow into a small mass that produces male and female parts. When the female part is fertilized by the male part, the mass grows into a new plant.

Conifer trees usually have needles for leaves and produce cones. For example, a pine tree produces pine cones. Seeds grow inside these cones, and are then released to grow into new trees when the cones open up.

These pine cones contain lots of seeds.

DID YOU KNOW?

Conifers called bristlecone pines are among the oldest living trees in the world. There is one growing in the White Mountains in California, USA, that is around 4,600 years old. In 1964, in Wheeler Peak, in Nevada, a bristlecone pine was cut down. It was later found to be 4,900 years old!

Flowers and seeds

By far the largest group of vascular plants is the flowering plants group. Over 80 per cent of plants are in this group. There is a wide range of different types of flowering plants, from tiny forget-me-nots to huge teak trees. They all have one thing in common: they all grow flowers. The job of the flowers is to make seeds.

Flowering plants make fruits when their seeds are ready. Some fruits attract animals that eat them. Some plants have dry fruits, which can be carried by the wind, and others have hooked fruits, which hitch rides on animals' coats. The seeds can be scattered and grow in new places.

This military macaw is eating pine fruits. The seeds come out in the animal's droppings, and can start to grow into a new plant.

How are animals classified?

The animal kingdom is another of the five major groups of living things on Earth. All animals belong to this kingdom, and they all have some basic similarities.

All animals need energy from food so they can move around and live. Unlike plants, animals can't make their own food. They have to eat something else to get their energy. Animals can move around. Animals also **mate** with other animals so they can have offspring.

DID YOU KNOW?

Scientists have guessed that there may be around seven million different species of animal on Earth, making the animal kingdom by far the largest of the five kingdoms. However, at the moment, only about two million animal species have been properly identified and named.

Although they look like plants, coral are in fact animals! They capture food from the sea water that washes over them. Unlike most other animals, when coral are adults, they don't move around.

Animal groups

The animal kingdom is split into two different groups: **vertebrates** and **invertebrates**. Vertebrates are animals with a backbone, and usually some other bony parts. These support the body of the animal. Dogs, crocodiles, seahorses, and parrots are all vertebrates.

Animals without backbones, such as insects, snails, crabs, spiders, and worms, are called invertebrates. Around 97 per cent of animal species are invertebrates.

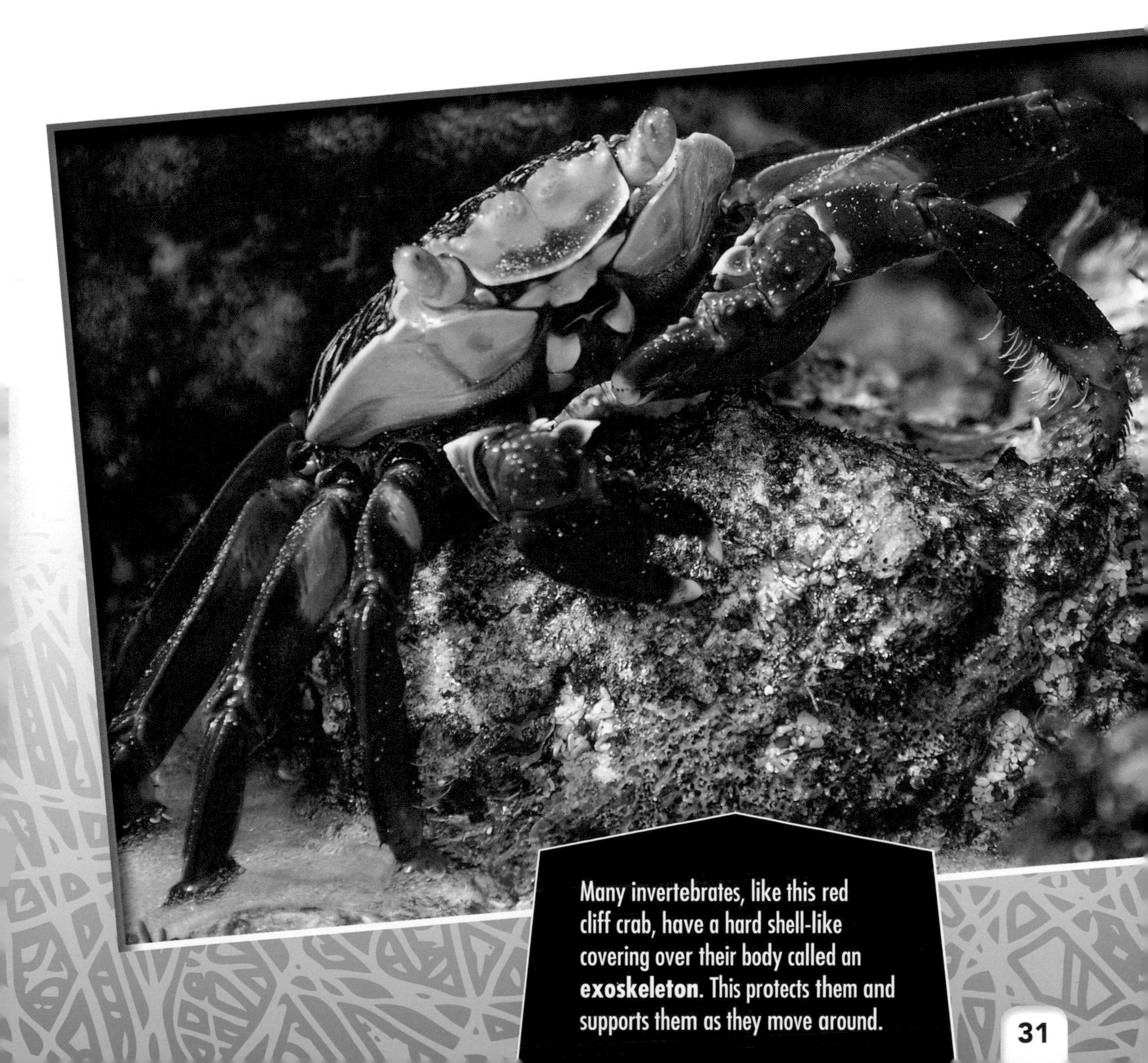

Many invertebrates, like this red cliff crab, have a hard shell-like covering over their body called an **exoskeleton**. This protects them and supports them as they move around.

Groups of vertebrates

Mammals are a group of vertebrates that are warm blooded. This means that they use energy from food to keep their bodies at the same temperature. They usually have some fur or hair. Most mammals give birth to live offspring rather than laying eggs. Mammals feed their offspring with milk from the mother.

Most mammals live on land, but some, such as dolphins and whales, live in the sea. They come up to the surface to breathe air. Humans are mammals. Bats are mammals that can fly.

Eureka moment!

Scientists are still discovering new species of mammals. In 2011, a snub-nosed monkey was discovered in Myanmar. This is an odd-looking animal with fleshy lips, an upturned nose, and a strange problem. When rain falls into their noses, it makes the animals sneeze, so they often spend wet days with their heads tucked between their knees.

Birds

Birds are another warm-blooded group of vertebrates. They have beaks, scaly legs, and bodies covered in feathers. They have wings, and most can fly. Some, such as ostriches, have very small wings and can't fly. Birds do not give birth to live offspring. Instead, they lay eggs. The young birds hatch out of the eggs when they are ready.

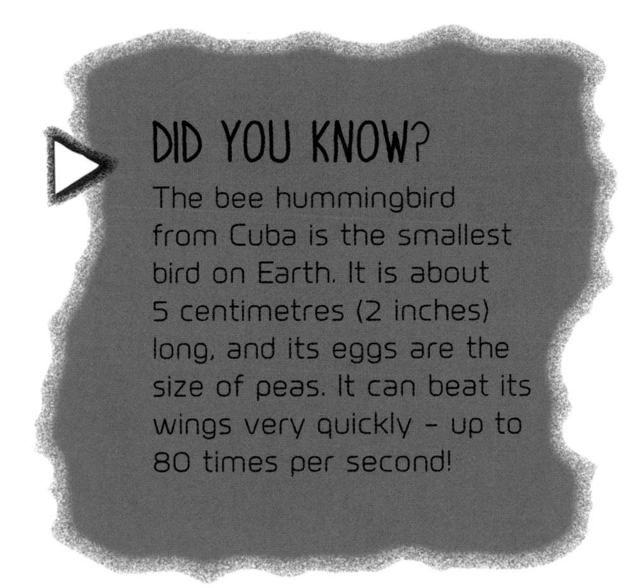

DID YOU KNOW?

The bee hummingbird from Cuba is the smallest bird on Earth. It is about 5 centimetres (2 inches) long, and its eggs are the size of peas. It can beat its wings very quickly – up to 80 times per second!

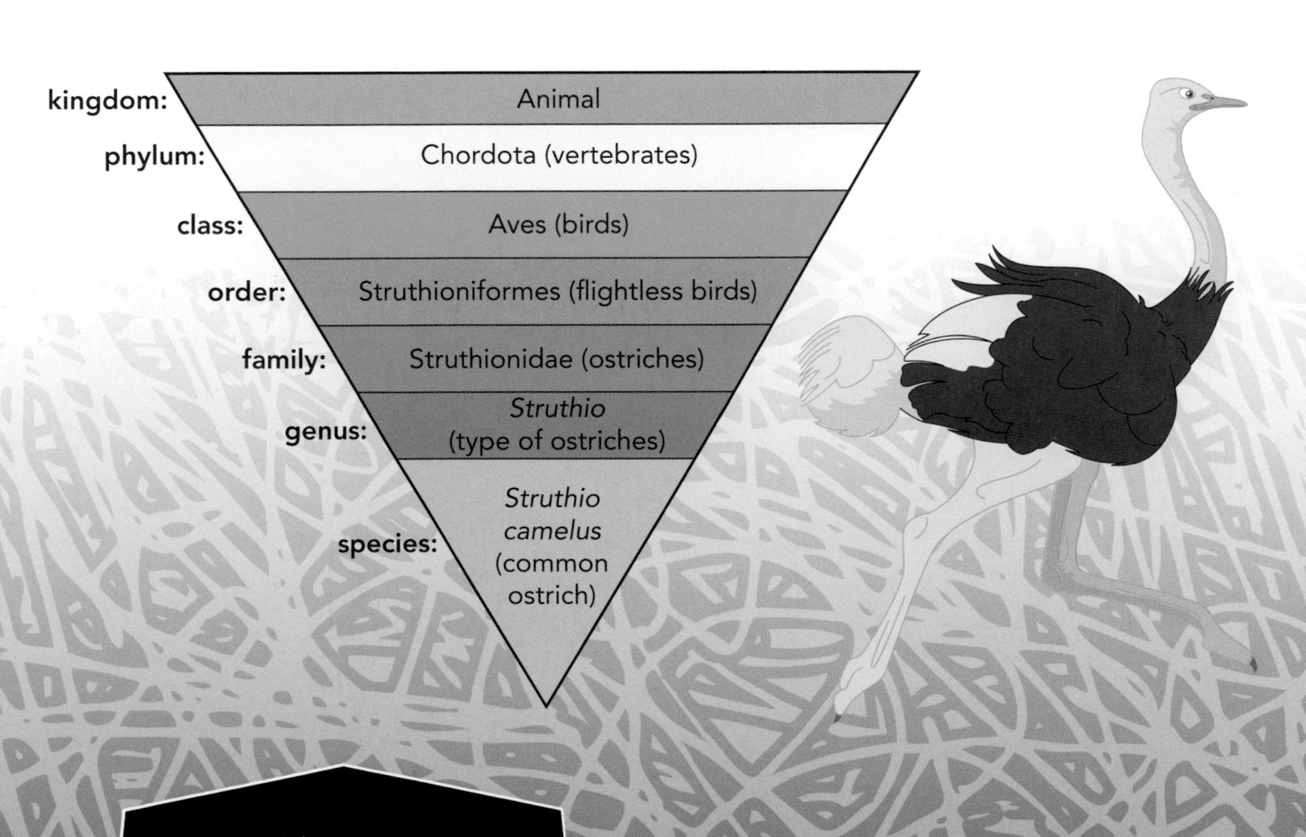

This is a classification pyramid for the common ostrich.

Cold-blooded animals

Cold-blooded animals do not use energy from food to keep their bodies at the same temperature. Their body temperature changes depending on the temperature of their environment. On warm, sunny days, cold-blooded animals become warm and more active than on cold days. There are three groups of cold-blooded vertebrates: fish, amphibians, and reptiles.

Fish live in water. They breathe using gills on the sides of their heads. Gills are feathery body parts that can take oxygen from the water. Most fish bodies are covered in scales. They swim using a side-to-side movement, and they have fins to help them move through the water.

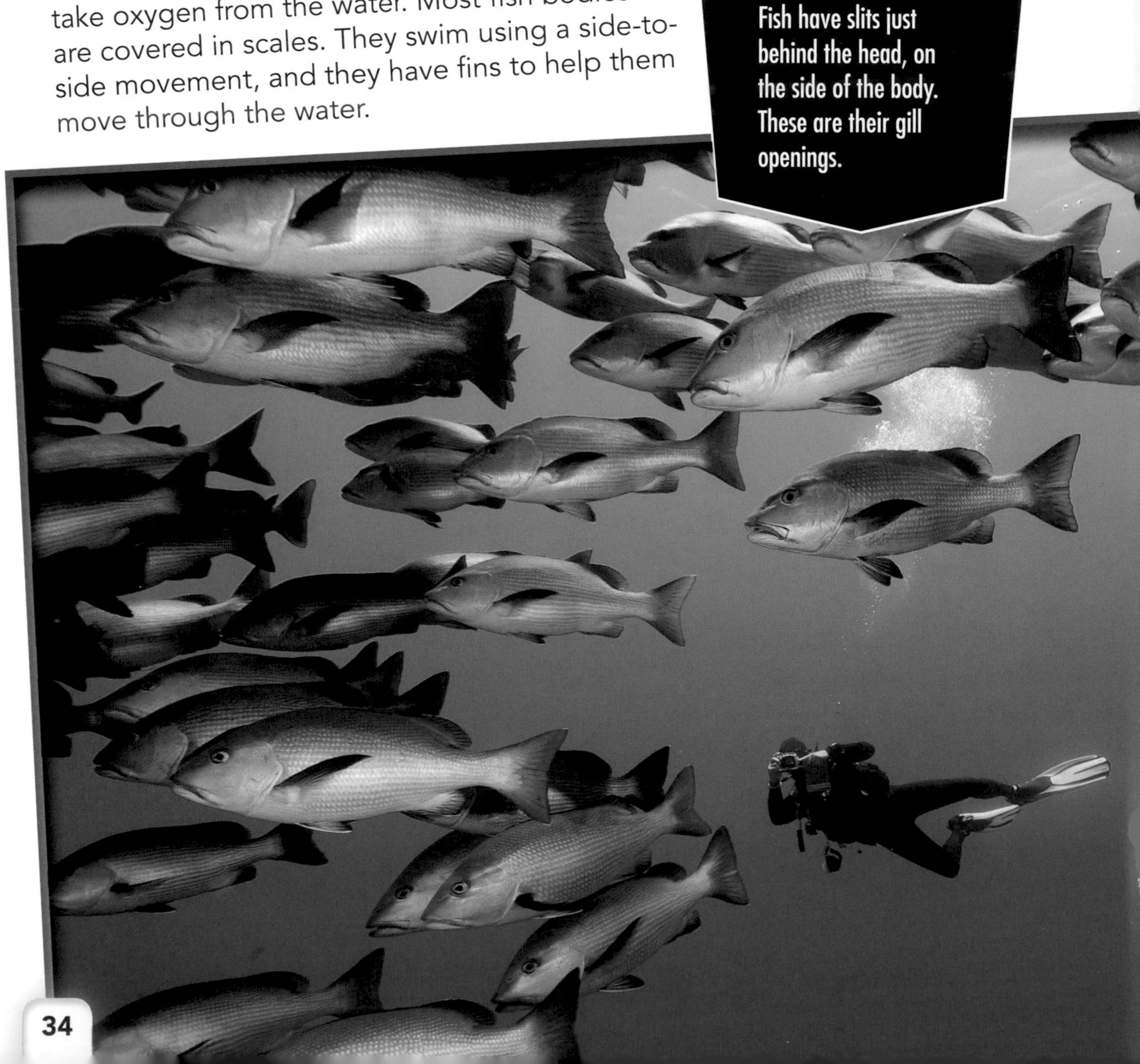

Fish have slits just behind the head, on the side of the body. These are their gill openings.

Amphibians and reptiles

Frogs, newts, and toads are amphibians. They all have slimy or warty skin. Amphibians live in water during the early parts of their lives. For example, frogs lay their eggs in water and young frogs, or tadpoles, live in water. Then, when they change into adults, they can live on land.

Reptiles have scaly bodies. Most of them lay eggs and some, such as snakes, have no legs. Lizards, crocodiles, turtles, tortoises, and alligators are all reptiles.

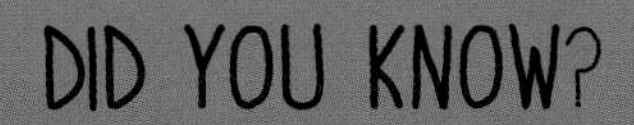

DID YOU KNOW?

Fossil remains of a huge snake have been found in a coal mine in Colombia. The snake was 14 metres (46 feet) long, and around 70 centimetres (28 inches) wide. It lived around 58 million years ago. It killed its prey by crushing it to death.

The thorny devil lizard lives in Australia. Its body is covered in lots of spikes, to make other animals think twice about eating it!

How can we identify species?

Sometimes it is quite easy to identify new species, especially large mammals. In 1992, a new large mammal called a saola was discovered in Vietnam. It has a backbone, four legs, hooves split in two, and two horns. Scientists worked out that it is a new species, related to cows. However, it can be a lot harder to identify new plants, or tiny invertebrates.

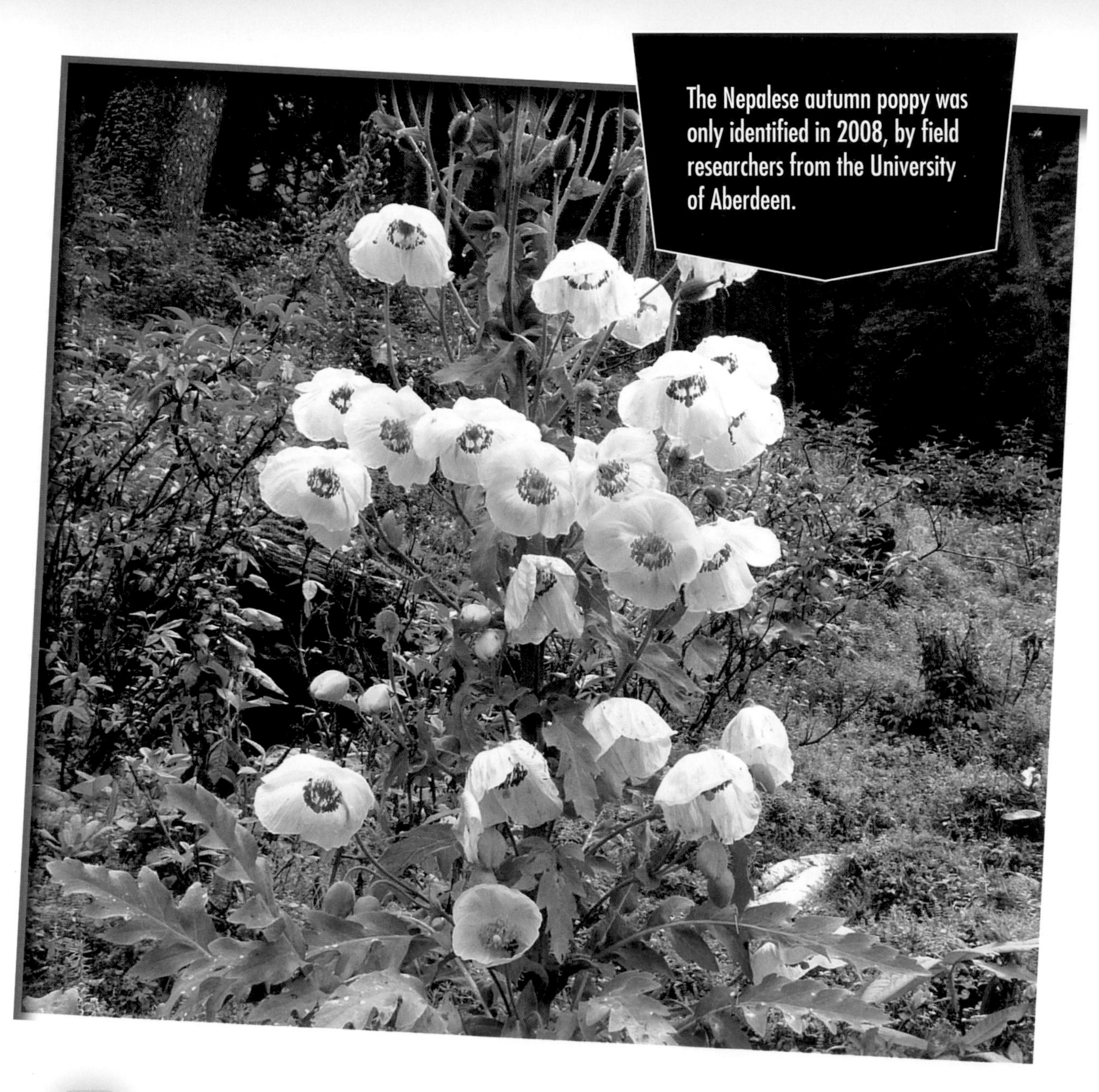

The Nepalese autumn poppy was only identified in 2008, by field researchers from the University of Aberdeen.

Looking for clues

Scientists study the appearance of a new plant or animal to try to work out what it is. Then they look at where it has come from, and how it behaves in its natural environment.

If the plant or animal is tiny, scientists can use microscopes to get a good look at it. They can also take a little bit from an animal (such as blood), or part of a plant. They can use this to work out its **DNA**. DNA is the information about the plant's or animal's genes. Scientists can compare this to DNA from other similar plants or animals.

DID YOU KNOW?

When a new species is discovered, it needs to be given a name. There are rules about naming species. The name must be in two parts, in Latin. The first part must say which group, or genus, the species belongs to. The second part is sometimes named after someone, often the person who discovered the new species.

This white-lined leaf frog is so tiny, it fits easily on a researcher's finger. Scientists are still able to study it by using microscopes and checking its DNA.

You might need a magnifying glass to see some small invertebrates.

What are classification keys?

If you want to try to identify plants and animals that are already known about, you can use a simple classification key. Many keys start at one point and ask a question about what you can see. For example, the question might be, "Does it have legs?" Depending on the answer, you move to a new section where you are asked another question, for example, "Does it have more than six legs?", and so on. Eventually you can work out what you are looking at.

You could try to identify some small woodland animals. Scoop up some leaves and soil from a woodland floor into a white tray, then pick out the leaves and larger bits of soil. You will be amazed at how many animals you will find there! They will probably all be invertebrates. If you use a simple woodland invertebrate classification key, you might be able to name them all.

DID YOU KNOW?

Charles Darwin (1809–1882) was one of world's most famous biologists. He spent a lot of time as a child bird-watching, exploring, and collecting beetles and other interesting creatures in his family's garden. He studied to become a doctor, and then a priest, but still he preferred to be outside collecting beetles!

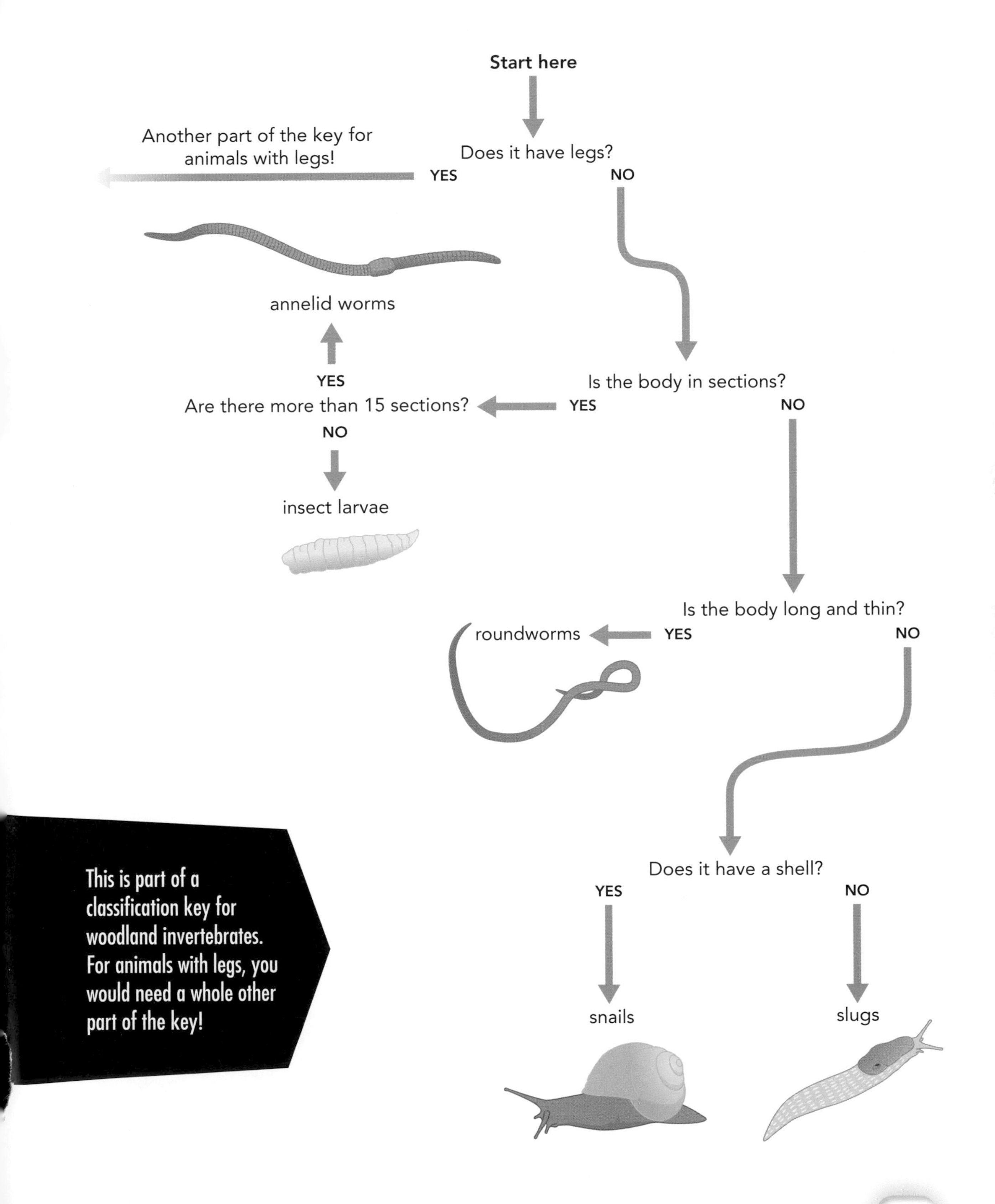

This is part of a classification key for woodland invertebrates. For animals with legs, you would need a whole other part of the key!

Try this!

Many keys used to identify things are called **dichotomous keys.** This means that you are given two choices at each stage in the key, and you have to decide which choice better fits the thing you are trying to identify. At the next stage, there are two more choices, and you again choose the better one. *Dichotomous* means "divided into two parts". You can create a dichotomous key to identify lots of things.

Prediction

Our class can create a dichotomous key to correctly identify each pupil.

What you need

- a class of school pupils
- a large room
- paper
- pens

What you do

1. As a class, decide on the first question to start identifying each person. It might be, for example, "Is the person male?" There are only two choices for this question. Write the question on a piece of paper, then write the two choices. Each pupil should move to the correct choice for them.

(2) Now within each group, think of the next question. Remember, it can only have two choices. It could be, "Does the person have blue eyes?" When you have decided on the question, everyone in each group should move to the correct choice.

(3) Continue to think of questions with only two choices for answers, until you end up with only one pupil in each group. You can now identify each pupil following the dichotomous key!

Conclusion

Our class managed to create a dichotomous key which we can use to correctly identify each pupil in the class.

What's next for life on Earth?

It is impossible to imagine just how many kinds of plants and animals there are on Earth that we know about, never mind those that we have not discovered yet! There is a huge range of different kinds, or diversity, of life on Earth.

It is important to be able to identify and name as many of Earth's different species as possible. If we know about species and where they live, we can protect them. We can study how species cope with changes, such as pollution or climate change. We can also control some species that affect us, by damaging food crops, for example.

Today's technology is making it easier for more people to identify and understand species. The internet means that people all over the world can share information and help each other identify plants and animals.

These weevil larvae are damaging the stems of a crop grown to produce oil. We need to identify species to know how to control them.

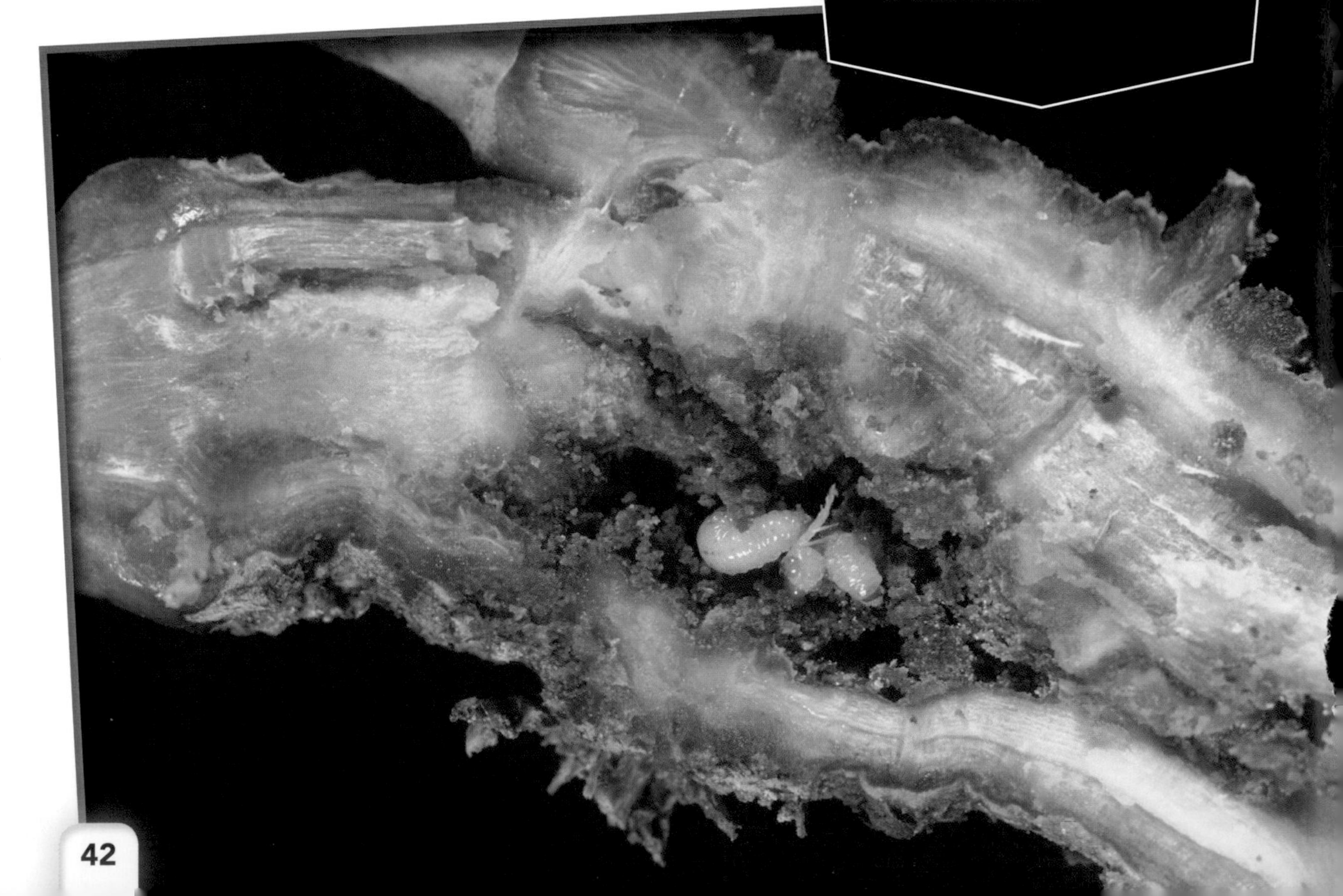

Losing species

Some human activity is killing off plant and animal species. Habitat destruction, over-fishing, pollution, climate change, and hunting are the main causes of species loss. But because we don't really know how many species there are on Earth, we don't really know how many become extinct every year! Scientists have estimated that the number of species lost every year could be as high as 2,000. We need to take action now, firstly to identify all of Earth's species and secondly to protect them.

WHAT'S NEXT?

The IUCN Red List is a list of all plants and animals and how much they are threatened by human activity. There are now around 20,000 threatened species on the list.

The pig-footed bandicoot once lived in large areas of Australia. Human farming practices brought changes to the bandicoot's habitat which led to its extinction in the 1950s.

Glossary

ancestor plant or animal from thousands of years ago to which a plant or animal from today is related

breed particular type of animal or plant within a species

characteristic physical or behavioural quality that a living thing can have or show

classification grouping things by the characteristics they have

classification system method of putting living things into groups according to the similar or different characteristics they have

dichotomous key series of questions with a choice of two answers that can be used to identify a plant or animal

DNA substance found in cells that contains information about the characteristics of a living thing. DNA is an abbreviation for **d**eoxyribo**n**ucleic **a**cid.

domestic animal animal that is looked after by humans. Farm animals are domestic animals.

environment conditions such as weather, plants, type of soil, and animals where an organism lives

evolution process by which species develop and change over a long period of time

exoskeleton hard covering on the outside of an invertebrate's body that protects and supports it

extinct species of plant or animal that has died out completely and no longer exists

fossil remains of something, usually an animal or plant, that lived a long time ago. Fossils are found inside rocks or in the earth.

gene code in the cells of living things that tell them how to grow and what to be like

genus (plural: **genera**) large group of different plants and animals that are closely related. There can be many different species in one genus.

habitat natural environment of an animal or plant

invertebrate animal that does not have a backbone

kingdom one of the five large groups that all living things can be put into

mammal warm-blooded animal that feeds its young with milk from the mother

mate come together to have offspring

natural selection process by which plants and animals that are best suited to their environment will survive best

nerve long fibre in an animal's body that carries messages to and from different parts

offspring child or young of a plant or animal

oxygen colourless and odourless gas found in the air

predator animal that hunts other animals for food

species type of living thing that can breed with another of the same species to produce offspring

trait characteristic that makes one thing different from another

variation amount of change or difference

vertebrate animal that has a skeleton inside its body, including a backbone

Find out more

Books

Animal Variation and Classification (Living Processes), Richard Spilsbury (Wayland, 2009)

Plant Variation and Classification (Living Processes), Carol Ballard (Wayland, 2009)

Websites

www.bbc.co.uk/bitesize/ks2/science/living_things/variation/read/1

On this BBC Bitesize website, you will find some basic information about variation, grouping things, and keys. You can play a variation game, and do a quiz to test yourself.

www.bbc.co.uk/schools/ks3bitesize/science/organisms_behaviour_health/variation_classification/revise1.shtml

This BBC Bitesize website has a lot of information about variation and classification. There is an activity and a test to help you understand some of the ideas.

www.doeni.gov.uk/niea/minibeast_for_web.pdf

This PDF is all about minibeasts, which are invertebrates. It has some activities to help you start your career as a taxonomist!

www.leics.gov.uk/wild_creepy_crawlies.pdf

This PDF has a key to help you identify types of woodlice. There is also lots of information about collecting and watching all sorts of woodland invertebrates. There are two larger keys at the end, to help you identify grassland invertebrates.

Organizations

The International Institute for Species Exploration

species.asu.edu/index

The Arizona State University in the United States has a department called the International Institute for Species Exploration. It aims to promote the use of modern technology – such as the internet – to identify more of Earth's species.

WWF
www.wwf.org.uk
This organization was set up in 1961. It aims to protect the diversity of plants and animals around the world. It campaigns for less pollution and better use of resources, and other ways of reducing the human impact on Earth.

Zoological Society of London
www.zsl.org
This charity is concerned with the conservation of animals and their habitats, all over the world.

Places to visit

Natural History Museum
Cromwell Road
London SW7 5BD
www.nhm.ac.uk

The Natural History Museum has many displays and activities to demonstrate the amazing diversity of life on Earth. You can learn about how plants and animals have changed over time, and how scientists work to discover all about the natural world.

Royal Botanic Gardens, Kew
26 West Park Road
Richmond
Surrey TW9 4DA
www.kew.org
The Royal Botanic Gardens in Kew has collections of plant species from all over the world. The researchers there work to conserve plants. They have created the Millennium Seed Bank in Wakehurst, Sussex, where they store the seeds of 10 per cent of the world's plants. They aim to have collected 25 per cent by 2020.

Go for a walk in your local nature park! Spend time looking closely at all the different animals and plants you can see. Can you identify any of them? Some of them, such as nettles, might be easy to identify. Others, such as insects, may not.

Index

amphibians 34, 35
ancestors 19
animal classification 30–35

bacteria 5
bears 15
bee hummingbirds 33
behaviours, different 11
birds 22, 29, 31, 33
breeds 22
bristlecone pines 28

camouflage 12
carbon dioxide 26
characteristics 18, 19, 22, 26
chimpanzees 15, 19
classes 23
classification 5, 18–35
classification keys 38, 39–41
classification systems 20–21
cold-blooded animals 34–35
conifers 27, 28
continuous variation 8, 9
coral 30
crabs 31
creating a classification system 24–25

Darwin, Charles 13, 38
dichotomous keys 40–41
dinosaurs 17
DNA 37
domestic animals 22

elephants 16
energy 4, 30, 32
environments 10, 11, 12, 13, 14, 17, 37
even-toed ungulates 18, 19
evolution 14–16, 17, 18, 19
exoskeletons 31
experiments 8–9, 24–25, 40–41
extinctions 17, 43

families 23
ferns 27, 28
fish 34
flowering plants 10, 11, 21, 27, 28, 29
fossils 16, 19, 35
frogs 35, 37
fruits 29
fungi 5

genera 23, 37
genes 7, 10, 11, 37

height 8–9
horses 10
humans 5, 6, 7–9, 11, 15, 19, 23, 32

identifying species 36–41, 42
inherited variations 7
invertebrates 31, 38, 39
IUCN Red List 43

kingdoms 23, 26, 27, 30, 31

Latin names 21, 37
leafy sea dragons 12
learning 10
levels of classification 23
Linnaeus, Carl 21
lizards 16, 35

mammals 17, 32, 36
Mendel, Gregor 7

naming species 4, 21, 37
natural selection 12–13, 14
new species 14, 15, 32, 36–37
non-living things 4, 23, 24–25
non-vascular plants 27
nutrients 27

orders 23
ostriches 33
oxygen 4, 26

pheasants 22
photosynthesis 26
phyla 23
plant classification 26–29
predators 12
primates 23
producers 26
protists 5

rainforest plants 26
reptiles 34, 35
rock squirrels 23

seeds 27, 28, 29
selective breeding 22
sharks 34
snakes 35
snub-nosed monkeys 32
species, definition of 22
species, threatened 43
species loss 17, 43
spores 27, 28
stick insects 12
survival of the fittest 13

traits 7, 10, 14, 18, 22
twins 6, 11

variation 4, 5, 6–17
vascular plants 27, 28–29
vertebrates 31, 32

warm-blooded animals 32–33
whales 14, 32